COLLABORATOR

Yussef El Guindi

I0140062

BROADWAY PLAY PUBLISHING INC
New York
www.broadwayplaypublishing.com
info@broadwayplaypublishing.com

COLLABORATOR

© Copyright 2017 by Yussef El Guindi

Cover art by Stephanie K Olson, photo by Jacob Lund

I S B N: 978-0-88145-696-7

First printing: March 2017

Book design: Marie Donovan
Page make-up: Adobe Indesign
Typeface: Palatino
Printed and bound in the U S A

COLLABORATOR was first produced by Macha Monkey Productions in Seattle (Kristina S Rowell, Artistic Director), opening on 28 April 2016. The cast and creative contributors were as follows:

CASS.. Hayley Guthrie

Director...Anita Montgomery
Set & costume design... Pete Rush
Lighting design ....Marcella Barbeau
Sound design.. Erin Bednarz
Stage manager.. Erin Dorn
Production managers ...... Ashley Ralph, Kristina S Rowell

CHARACTER & SETTING

CASS

A bed

DEDICATION

For my sisters and brother, Fatma, Zein and Zaki.

ACKNOWLEDGMENTS

Thanks to Anita Montgomery for her amazing talents as a director. Always a pleasure to work with you. Thanks to Kristina S Rowell and Macha Monkey Productions for taking a chance with this play. To the incomparable Hayley Guthrie for taking on such a challenging role and doing a wonderful job with it. And to all the folks at West of Lenin Theater for hosting this production.

(A bed on stage. A woman, CASS, *enters. She is dressed in pajamas. She addresses the audience.)*

Part 1

CASS: Thank you for coming this evening. That's very sweet of you to come tonight and spend some time with me. I know there had to have been other things to tempt you, so the fact that you chose to come, thank you. I'm sure in the course of our short time together we'll warm up to each other. I'm certainly going to do my best to warm up to you. I hope you'll throw some love my way as well.

However badly this goes. However bored you might become.

Please don't walk out if you're bored. No matter how unbearable what you're watching is, please don't. This isn't a big enough space not to notice you leave. You will undermine my confidence, just a little.
And do you really want to do that? Even to a stranger? No. You're theater people. You people go to the theater. That means you're sensitive and caring just by being here. I know theater people aren't immune from being mean. We're inclined to be civilized about things, yes. I'm not expecting you to throw rotten vegetables at me. And thank you ahead of time for that.

Then again we civilized people can be—we can be pretty passive-aggressive, no? Just because you might refrain from throwing a tomato at me doesn't mean the impulse won't arise.

(Whispering to them in a mock aside:)

It might. Hang out. We'll see.

(Back to normal volume)

I think that's why we secretly admire the people who say "fuck it" and do it anyway. That thing we wouldn't dare think of doing ourselves. Those people have no shame; or do a good job of not caring. We secretly love that about them.

(Animated at the thought)

Can you imagine living without any shame whatsoever? I feel twenty pounds lighter just thinking about it. "Fuck it" is a great motto to have in your back pocket. Most of the time. Other times you probably do need a teeny bit of shame, just so you don't become too obnoxious.

You know what: I'm being too controlling. If you want to leave, go for it. Not now. I'm just starting. But later, if you want to go, do it. I won't flip out. I'll wish you well as you turn your back on me. Seriously, no hard feelings. But if you do leave, could you do it, you know, quietly. Crouched down, so you don't block anyone's view.

We'll stop the show momentarily, so don't worry about overlapping me in anyway. We'll stop everything so nobody gets distracted by your pointed leaving.

And then, just so you know, I will probably critique your exit behind your back; because at that point you'll become part of this evening's entertainment. I'm going to get critiqued, so why shouldn't you—if you enter my show by leaving it. I will deem your exit either intriguing, or—mundane. A disappointing departure. "The person exited much as other patrons have exited before him. With little sensitivity or reason for doing so. Needs work."

A quick bit of important business before we start. The
(Making quotation marks around the word:)
"collaborator" on this piece is male. He is aware of the
challenges that poses as we delve into the material,
as you'll see. So he wants that mentioned up front.
Together we've decided to stage this with me in a bed
wearing this. Though I stress it was me initially who
suggested all of this, what I'm wearing, the bed.

I could be seated in a chair, instead of lounging about
on these silky sheets. A chair has been placed on stage
with a rather frumpy dressing gown in case I start
feeling too exposed. I doubt I'll need it. I'm the one
who suggested that I should start shedding an article
of clothing if ever I feel I am losing your attention. That
freaked him out. Given what we're going to talk about.
But I've written in red marker in my script to remind
myself, "Don't be afraid to be crass or vulgar." Even
as we dissect these very things. The performer in me
simply won't allow you to get bored if I can help it. I
am not above cheap tricks to keep your attention. For
example, if need be:
(She lets something fall off her shoulder in a mock,
provocative move. Also, mock French accent.)
Voilà. A preview. Or:
(Hikes her sleepwear a little to expose a part of her thigh. She
sweeps her hand over her thigh.)
Le thigh.
(Back to normal accent)
Yes?
I'm not saying this will necessarily pique your interest.
I hope it does.

To sum up: I am not only happy you should look at
me, I'd be upset if you didn't. I have worked hard at
this performance. You are encouraged to stare.

Which brings me to the first point of this evening's presentation, which I've been talking about, but let me spell it out again: Ladies and gentleman, I would love for you to look at me, even with desire. I want you to gobble me up. Eyes up front and nowhere else. If your mind strays, take me along with you. If you're thinking about drinks after the show, imagine ordering one for me. I'll have a Vodka martini with a lemon twist, please.

That's how much I want you to gobble me up.

Because let's be honest: I am going to measure my worth by how much attention you pay me tonight. As an artist, yes, but that's so tied up with how I see myself, that I am going to end up measuring everything else about me as well. And if I don't measure up because I fail tonight, that judgement will double-down on me and gnaw, just gnaw at me until there's nothing left but a cannibalized and self-digested me that's just lying here like a big talking stool. Like someone took a big dump on this bed and that dump is me, talking to you; and later, crying in my own bed, all alone and semi-suicidal because you hated what I did. That's how badly you'll make me feel.

Or: if it's a positive experience, and I feel the love from you (and if you don't feel it, don't force it, seriously, but if you do), then the streets I walk back home on will feel like trampolines under my feet. I will bounce back home to my bed and smile myself to sleep— waking up to unexplained pats on my back from a hand that's still too delirious to sleep.

And my question is: What the hell is that?

I am personally embarrassed by this. This needy, greedy—greedy thirst for attention. Oh my god, what the hell is that? My goodness.

Sure: some things are obvious in my case, I'm an actor.
Everybody wants to do well in their chosen profession
and success is measured in mine by eye-balls: How
many there are, and whether or not they're directed at
me. My neediness is not emotional, it's professional.
It's not that I want to be the center of attention, it's
simply part of my job description.

In fact, if I wasn't concerned about that, I would rightly
be accused of being self-centered. Focused only on
my artistic expression. Nothing to do with trying to
connect with you. Those kinds of artists are hostile to
audiences. It's all about rehearsal and self-discovery
for them. You're the interruption. I, on the other hand,
I want to give back. You're the star attraction. I'm here
to create an enjoyable evening for you. "How can I
serve you?" is my philosophy.

Really, it's all about you. When people pretentiously
speak of an artist giving of themselves, and those
stories you hear of artists who kill themselves, and
friends will say by way of explanation,
(Concerned friend voice:)
"Well, you know, she just gave and gave until she
hadn't any more to give."
(Back to normal voice)
There is some truth to that. You are not just taking me
in, I'm taking you in. With every shift in your seat.
With every cough. Every time you look down at your
program. Even more than the obvious signs, I'm really
just plugged in to all those things you can just feel in
an audience. This isn't just me speaking. I'm—trying
to create an intimacy that won't really work until I can
feel you here with me. In bed.
(Perhaps she pats the bed?)
Between the sheets.

So to speak.

So:…

won't you please slide into bed with me?

(A beat)

Part 2 (A)

CASS: So I'm walking home one night. It was after a
performance of this old French farce I was in a while
ago. And…

*(There is a glass of water on a bed stand beside her. She will
take a sip from it whenever she needs to.)*

I hadn't removed my make up. I was rushing home to
curl up on the couch with a bowl of popcorn and talk
on the phone with this guy I was seeing at the time. I
don't know why I always made popcorn whenever I
had one of my epic chats with this guy. I've never done
that with other guys. No: I have. Okay, it's a thing.
Two other guys. I think as you're starting out on your
dating life early on (this is a quick aside before I get to
what happened that night), as you start your dating
life, the people you go out with are like these…
you know Virgil in Dante's Inferno? Everything is
so new to you when you start out in dating-land,
that the partners you pick end up being like these—
guides—into uncharted territory, kind of. Of course
they also may be the ones creating the hell they're
guiding you into. But at an early age you make so
many discoveries about yourself through the person
you're dating that the other person is a kind of guide
into these new phases of life you're beginning. Like—
well, like watching the movie of your life take shape.
So of course popcorn seemed to go with that. Plus
everything feels so epic early on in your love life. Your
emotional highs and lows, sex, it all feels so—operatic,
and world changing.

Later, I learned he hated hearing me eat popcorn.
Didn't say anything at the time because he thought he
was in love, and let it pass. But as time went on, nausea
trumped love, apparently.

B.S., of course. Yes, the little things we overlook
when we're in love become the icebergs that sink the
relationship later on, blah blah, but that isn't true
either. Who doesn't have one or two things that irritate
your partner. We're human. We have annoying laughs,
or we chew our food too loudly, or whatever. Flaws
are us.

No, the truth is he found someone else, banged her,
and then pulled this popcorn excuse out of his ass as
one of several reasons for breaking up with me. That
drove him into the arms of another woman. My eating
popcorn over the phone. Drove him to have sex with
someone else.

God, men and their penises. For goodness sake, get a
grip. My collaborator has tried to explain what it's like
to have a penis. Not to contradict him, but I have a sex
drive. I've even been accused of being slutty, which I'll
get to, but why is it I can keep my vagina tucked away
and you can't do the same with your privates?

No penis envy here. Nope. If male genitalia makes you
that ethically challenged, keep them. I don't mean to be
overly critical. Men's equipment have been a source of
pleasure for me. Even the men they're attached to have
been fun. Most men are lovely. Just not the one who
had a huge fucking problem with my eating popcorn
over the phone.

Part 2 (B)

CASS: Anyway. So I'm walking home one night after this performance. Where I played this flirty French maid who gets hit on by the men in this family. Especially by the grandfather. The humor's supposed to arise from the antics of this over-sexed grand dad who poses no real sexual threat because of his age. Which allows the audience to laugh at his aggressive behavior. At the end he smacks her bottom so hard, and gets so excited by the act, that he has a heart attack and dies. The maid is suspected of foul play and a police officer is called in. The officer says:

(She plays the characters with different French accents.)

(Officer) I still do not understand, *mademoiselle*. He had a heart attack after a simple smack of your bottom?

(Maid) Just so, *monsieur*. I was polishing the silver when I heard the steps of Monsieur Philippe behind me. I thought he was going for the cognac, but instead, it was not the bottle he wanted to hit.

(Officer) He smacked it and
(Makes sound)
"fft", died?

(Maid) Yes, *monsieur*. I am not responsible for the effects my bottom has on others.

(Bernard) Her bottom has been a source of much chaos in the family, officer.

(Back to regular accent) The young son in the family pipes in.

(Bernard, French accent) That bottom had a hand in murdering my grandfather, I am sure of it. I demand she be locked up.

(Back to regular accent) There's a final bit where the officer insists on replaying the events that led to the old

man croaking and the maid has to demonstrate. He still doesn't see how that could possibly have been a fatal blow and asks, because it is a French farce, if it wasn't more like this, and he hits her on her bottom.
(Slaps her hand to make the sound)
My character says "*non, non*, it was more like this."
(Slaps her hand to make the sound)
She hits him on his bottom. The young son and the rest of the family have different takes on the fatal blow, and everyone starts hitting each other's bottoms.

Curtain. End of play.

There's also a hint the young police officer and the maid may be falling for each other as they exchange meaningful glances as they smack each other's bottoms. Years of conservatory training, mountains of student debt, and here I am at last applying my craft in a professional setting. That play really did make me question my career choice, I have to admit.

But I did meet Andrew. The actor who played the police officer. (This is all of a piece, I promise. These asides all lead to Rome, to this incident that happened that night, so patience, please, as I briefly tell you about Andrew.)

Andrew.
Oh, the twisted paths our hearts take when lust rears its head. Soon after we started dating—this was before what happened that night walking home—soon after we fell into bed, he playfully reenacted the spanking. We giggled about it and made love.
The next night, much the same: ass spanking, giggles and sex. Until he wanted to do it again and I began to think, you know: the whole humor thing around the spanking has pretty much run its course. All the comic irony about life imitating art was funny the first time, less the second, and now—now my ass was just sore.

Plus I still didn't really know him that well. Getting
naked with him was still a big deal. It's not like we'd
been seeing each other for years and now needed to
spice up our sex life. I still got a lot of mileage from
simply using tongue and lips. Kissing is not a prelude
for me. Throw in a little heavy petting and I am good
for the night.

But he loved the kink, I came to discover. In the
beginning he jokingly explained he was staying in
character: "And don't you think the police officer is
secretly a fetishist? What with the uniform and the
handcuffs," he asked.
(Teasing voice:)
"So what do you have in mind, big boy?" I said.

"Oh, I don't know…I bet he's into rope. Lots of rope."
(Teasing voice:)
"Oh, rope, huh," I said.
*(She puts her hands behind her back, or crossed in front of
her. French accent)*
"I surrender. Do with me what you will."
(Regular accent.)
And so, he did.

Let me jump ahead and say nothing bad happened. He
tied me up with his belt. Next time with a rope. Chains
after that. You know, the kind of thing that some
people regard as today's version of heavy petting. In
about ten years time, people will view all this kink the
way we view those 50s movies of teenagers necking
in the backseat. They'll say, "Oh, how cute. Do you
remember when those fetishes were a big deal? How
innocent those times were."

Anyway, I wasn't into it. The rope chaffed, the chain
was scary, and before the French farce was over, we
amicably parted. He's now come out as a full-blown
S&M practitioner, and makes his services available for

swingers who want to spice things up. Good for him.
If it's consensual, and you're adults, go for it. It just
wasn't for me. Plus, I was a little lost with the strange
dynamic taking shape. We went from playing our
characters to, well, other kinds of role playing. First I
was a kidnapped princess. Then a spy held hostage.
Then a slave forced to cater to the sexual whims of her
master.

Again, you know, as they say, the biggest sex organ
you got is your brain; and if that's what fired his up…

Though—

it did make me wonder. Because something about it
felt very…familiar. Like I was reenacting something
that I sometimes feel is always—playing around the
edges of my everyday life.
That is relegated to the edges for good reason. Then
again, there was something honest about his desires.
An honest expression of that something that always
seem to hover just out of sight. At least for me. A thing
that wants to crawl into bed with you, and just—
declare itself…
On the other hand, he was a great kisser, I have to
admit. It's a shame that became less and less important
to him.

I really—really do love to kiss.
I almost don't need to do anything else.
That first meeting of lips is so—powerful to me.
Everything else feels almost like a let down after that
initial burst of intimacy. It's kind of shocking just
how intimate a kiss is. I could go on and on about my
very first kiss. I won't. Except—when it happened,
I couldn't believe it was happening. It's no wonder
books are written about magic, and spells, witches
and warlocks when the simple acts in our lives can
transform even our ordinary days into something

amazing. And enchanted. One moment you're hanging
out on the back porch with this boy, like I was when I
was fifteen, and the next—that moment you dreamed
would one day happen is happening.

Okay, I will tell you about it; it's related, I promise.
So I was fifteen and this boy from school, who'd come
over for a class project, he wanted—well it was clear he
wanted to kiss me. I could tell because his voice started
dropping. You know, like a bunch of frogs had jumped
down his throat. Any small talk he was capable of
had suddenly dried up. And he was looking at me
with that intensity that comes just before something
like your very first kiss ever is about to happen. He
was trying to be cool, but I could tell something was
like, welling up inside of him. And I don't mean just
sexually. Neither of us had kissed before. I could tell
that from the look in his eyes. Such—pleading. And
fear. And desire. And even more fear. I wish I could go
back and just hug that boy for the terror he must have
felt. And hug me. The terrified me. We were both about
to experience something neither of us had prepared
for. Fantasized about, yes. But fantasy is no substitute
for rehearsal. Neither of us were prepared. How could
we have been. This was our future, and you can't
rehearse emotions you've never experienced before.
Well, you can, but even make-believe can't prepare you
for a moment like this.

I don't know what my expression was, or how he was
interpreting it, but he must have known it was now or
never. He lowered his eyes to my lips. He leaned in,
and....

Amazing that teeny, little distance between two people
on a first kiss. I could go on and on about that.
But I won't. Except to say nomads setting out to
cross the Sahara dessert—pilgrims making their way
to Mecca have shorter distances to travel than two

kids leaning in for a first kiss. With Mecca you know where you're heading, but with this? This was more like Columbus heading for the Indies. Planning for the Indies, but ending up some where completely different.

(Beat)

(Note: if the lights had been dimming during the above tale of a first kiss, leaving a sole spotlight on the bed, they now go up again.)

Part 2 (C)

CASS: So I'm walking home after another performance of this French farce. My apartment is not too far from the theater, and I see these two guys up head walking towards me. It's around eleven P M. I'm rushing home to curl up on the couch for a bowl of popcorn and a chat, as I said. Andrew had offered to walk me home. And—oh, just so you don't think I'm a complete slut, the Andrew fling ended three weeks into the run. There wasn't any overlap with the new boyfriend. I'm on the prudish side of things, just so you know. And yes, you can be a prude and still be okay with other people's bondage needs. I'm speaking ethically here. Doing right by others.

Anyway. Two guys heading towards me. A little alarm bell went off, as it will in these situations. I was wary, but not scared. Just—that internal radar that scans for possible dangers? It beeped.

Nothing really to be afraid of.

But it was a narrow sidewalk on a street at night with nobody else around. Plus they had that boisterous energy of guys out for a good time. All very peacockish, if you know what I mean. Joking, laughing loudly. Doing that guy thing where some testosterone-fueled competition or something was clearly in play. I say "clearly" because apart from getting my male collaborator's take on this, you can just tell when guys are preening in front of each other. There's a guy version of what girls do in front of each other, and this felt like that.

I could have been totally wrong. They might've been discussing their grandmothers for all I know. But it didn't have that vibe.

Even as I told myself not to jump to any conclusions.

I could've crossed the street. Or turned around and headed back to the more crowded main street. But now I'm doing battle with the good citizen in me. The one that doesn't want to pre-judge. Who cringes when that primitive part of you jumps to certain stereotypes.

There's crime in cities, sure. But if you're paranoid about everything you'll end up miserable. "Yay, I'm safe; even as I go through life terrified."
Take precautions, yes. You're crazy if you don't. But I just think, personally, that you have to err on the side of trust. Otherwise you're condemning yourself to a kind of jail.

And this was not a bad neighborhood.
Plus I'm walking home. I'm not going into some dicey area where women might get the blunt end of some male crap.

In addition: fuck this fear that I'm feeling.
"Fuck that" is not the same as "fuck it", but it's a close cousin.
So yeah, fuck that.
And fuck those guys for making me feel afraid even though they may be discussing their grandmothers.
And fuck me for sinking into the very stereotypes about guys that creates such a fear in the first place.

I'm sure they're lovely guys.

I think one of them was even wearing a tie-dye T-shirt. (I'm giving you my illogical thoughts at the time.) And sandals. That gave me immediate relief. (God, our prejudices.) But I actually thought: tie-dye plus sandals equals—I know there's no logic to this, but I thought: I don't know, maybe mellow stoner dudes? Or art lovers? Or, and: maybe those two guys are just coming back from seeing a play. And that energetic male thing is really them discussing the play in a passionate way. There was a theater not too far from where we were that was showing "Hedda Gabler" at the time. Maybe their loud conversation was about that:

"God, I love Ibsen."

"I know, Ibsen rocks."

"Hedda Gabler's so cool, man."

"Fuck yeah. I think I prefer Ibsen to Beckett."

"No."

"Yes."

"Apples and oranges, man. Apples and fucking oranges."

That is the conversation they might have been having. Now that I had identified their clothing options. I think I even heard one of them say something about a woman performing on stage.

All of this is bouncing around my head. And you know how I spoke of that first kiss? How the distance between me and that boy as he leaned in felt like forever? This was kind of similar for the opposite feeling. It wasn't the suspense of something wonderful about to happen. But the opposite. Where the best outcome would be that nothing happened.

At this point, one of the guys coming towards me locks
eyes with me. The other guy also catches my eyes.
"Catches" is a good word. I did feel kind of caught in
that moment. Or, I'd arrested their attention.
Something I thrive on normally, as I mentioned. All
eyes on board for the Cass express.
And normally the idea of people stopping their talk
at the sight of me, as they did, would be like manna
to my fragile ego. Who doesn't have the little princess
in us who dreams of a world that shushes as you pass
by; and then hears whispers of admiration afterwards.
I'm still trying to wrap my mind around that thirst to
be—noticed. This thing of, "We're social animals" just
doesn't feel like a good explanation anymore. This feels
more like a
soul need.
A deep,
nurture-me-with-attention, or I-will-wilt-and-die need.
Why invisibility feels like death, like exile in your own
body, I don't know.
How ugly—really. It can get quite ugly that thirst.
How more relaxed we'd be if we just had the
confidence to be wholly ourselves without needing
others to prop us up.
Saints can do that, supposedly.
Who needs others when you have God for company.
The mad, also, mad people.
You have all sorts of people populating your mind
when you're mad. But for the rest of us…
Or maybe we'd drift apart if we didn't need other
people's attention. The way galaxies are drifting apart
until our universe is supposed to die a horribly cold
death.
Gravity is good. Experiencing that tug towards
each other is a good thing, normally. Not when a
predator falls on its prey. Or three bodies are coming

towards each other and one of them feels irrationally
threatened. Because when I'm close enough to really
see them gazing at me, I immediately experience a kind
of—
well,
stage fright.
I am truly in a bizarre line of work.
Because what I experience every night is fear. An
exhilarating fear, yes, but fear nonetheless. I almost
go into a fugue state when I walk on, those first nights
before an audience.
I, Cass, go on a kind of life support as I have a kind of
out-of-body experience where the emotional journey is
truly unknown. Even though I'm dutifully following a
script.

Under the gaze of those two men, the same thing.
Except that my vague disappearance that sometimes
happens when I go on stage felt even more enveloping.
At the same time, I felt painfully self-conscious.
Disappeared and too self-conscious.
I hadn't bothered to remove my stage make-up.
I had heavy mascara that made my eyes pop.
I had blush that highlighted my cheek bones.
My lips alone felt like a separate prop with the red
lipstick. Every part of me felt like a separate prop.
My hair, my eyes. A little make-up to accentuate the
cleavage.
Everything was just popping at that moment. Pop,
pop, pop.
(With each pop, she refers to a different body part, the last
being her thighs.)
I was also in summer hem-line mode, so my thighs
could feel what little breeze there was.

Thirty feet away and I just know one of them is going
to say something to me.

I can feel it.

It's going to be nasty.

I even see his lip starting to curl.

He's going to verbally poke me and show off to his friend.

The other guy looks less sure.

The shy type.

He must know his friend well-enough to know he's going to use me to show off.

And the shy type looks like he might get in on the action too.

Because he's too weak to know he has a choice. Not if he doesn't want to be labelled lame. There is also something called chivalry.

A little patronizing, but preferable.

He could stop his friend if he tries something.

But chivalry isn't the name of the game here.

Measuring how big your dick is is.

I really think in these types of situations men should just own up to what this is really all about.

They should just turn to each other and say, "This isn't about her, it's about you, man."

When you scratch beneath the surface, we women have nothing to do with it.

We are just props for the buried desires of these kinds of macho guys who really just want to take their dicks out and you know, measure them against each other. Maybe even play with them in front of each other.

So do it already and leave us out of it.

I have had this somewhat confirmed by my male collaborator. We quibble over details, but I think he basically agrees about what's going on when guys sexualize a woman in front of each other. The subtext of it all. The underneath stuff.

Think of the relief if men could just own up to it and
say: "Guys: I know we're about to say something to
this woman that will try and prove just how manly we
are. But I think what this is actually about is measuring
our manhood. So instead of being dicks and saying
something nasty, I think we should just find a quiet
room where we can take out our privates and, you
know, share. And not be afraid to see where the
moment takes us.

Think of all the weight and pressure falling off if guys
were that honest:

"Why Robert, look at your privates. I've always
wondered what they looked like whenever you'd
whistle at a woman passing by and called her a sexy
bitch. I could not but help wonder from whence
such bravado came, and here it is. That which you
threatened to whip out."

"Yes, Sam, here is my penis. In truth, I wanted you
especially to admire it. I thought the best way to do
that would be to insult a woman. You can touch it."

"Thank you, Robert. Would you object if I took it a step
further and blew you?"

"I dared not hope. You may, please. But only if I can
return the favor."

"The pleasure is all mine."

Love would spread. If guys were that honest. Women
would be safe to walk the streets at night. We should
not be afraid to talk about this.

But that is not going to happen tonight.
No.
Those guys are going to take out their metaphorical
privates and show me, and each other, just how huge
they are.

And sure enough, the one whose lips had started to curl says, "Hey, you want to suck my dick?"

I should say a few seconds earlier I had put myself in emotional lockdown, bracing myself for such a comment. I avoided their gaze as I steeled myself to walk right through them, feeling they would have to part if I stayed my course.
And they did.
I could see the shy one had that nervous glee of a hyena—
that flips between excitement at seeing its prey, and fear it might all go terribly wrong.

By this time I realized they were definitely not theater people. They had not come back from seeing Ibsen. They looked like Middle Class brats out to show their education wasn't going to get in the way of all that Neanderthal bluster that was apparently their gender's right.

The brash one lets the back of his hand brush against my thigh as I walk past. Not a grab. Just casual enough so he could deny he meant to do it, if he had to.
This same guy whispers, like he's sticking his tongue in my ear,
"You won't regret it."

Now:...

There are many things in life I have regretted doing. But just as interesting are those things I'm sure I will never regret not doing. Like skydiving.
I know I won't because it's an insane thing to do. I'm with gravity on this one: "You will go splat if your chute doesn't open; so don't fuck with me."
I would also like to try "exotic eating." Where you're served fried cockroaches and tarantulas, just to say I'd

done it. Does it all taste like poultry? I'll never know, because that also seems like an insane thing to do.

But for sure I know I will never look back on that night and think, "If only I had taken that guy up on his offer. If I had just seized the moment, carpe diem, and sucked him off. Aagh, regret."
I also knew I'd kick myself if I didn't say something. I was no longer afraid at this point, now that I was in it. I was just pissed that I'd feared the worst. And pissed these guys had the nerve to be as stereotypical as I feared they'd be.

Really, part of me wanted to say, "Aren't you embarrassed? Couldn't you have risen above the stereotypes people have of your gender in a moment like this and made me feel ashamed for thinking the worse of you?"

Instead, what comes out of my mouth is, "Sure. Where would you like me to suck it?"

Physically I am now a few steps away from them.
We've both stopped to look at each other.
I have to say I hadn't really thought this through.
There was no one-two punch.
I was simply angry enough to call their bluff.
I wanted to say, "I may look like a French maid who gets her bottom spanked every night, but right now I am channeling Hedda fucking Gabler, and I am about to hand your asses back to you, motherfuckers".

At some point.
Just as soon as my brain catches up with my big mouth.
You will wilt from the knee-capping sarcasm I am about to inflict on you.
Your little pee-wees will shrivel from the shame I am going to make you feel.

"Want to suck my dick?" Really?

The shy one is sufficiently gobsmacked by my apparent agreement to suck dick.

The one who invited me to fellate him also looks thrown. This wasn't how it was supposed to go from his perspective, I'm sure. He was supposed to verbally stick his finger into one of my "orifices" and then cackle over his bravado. High-five his friend.

The walking orifice, me, wasn't supposed to reply. Sex objects don't talk back.

They don't challenge,

they comply.

What the hell was this bitch saying? Wait: Was that a yes? Could I be so lucky?

I know such women on porn sites exist, but do they also walk the better neighborhoods of Seattle? *(Other cities can be substituted.)*

Or could she really be a

prostitute?

I see his eyes light up.

For a second I feel I've stepped in it.

I'd challenged him, and for the brief moment he was thrown, it felt good. I had trumped his bravado with a middle finger of my own. I had metaphorically bent his offered penis back to him and said, "No, you suck it, asshole, and see how that feels." But any satisfaction I felt left as I see him actually look at me like I might fulfill some sexual fantasy of his. He'll have a story to tell. Maybe even bragging rights.

What's interesting to me is that, at that moment, for the first time—it felt like a first because of the added feeling of real, physical threat, but it can't have been a first;

but what felt like a first was that I truly felt in that
moment like
...meat—
in the eyes of another person.

Which is odd, given my profession.

I know we're meat. Existentially we're all meat.
Especially when things in our lives will slam us back
into our bodies, like hunger, or desire. And the burst
of pleasure that comes when those bodily needs are
satisfied in a way that feels like a welcome release from
the neck-up lives we live. The body is marvelous. This
marvelous body that desires,
and is sometimes desired right back, if you're lucky.

You know...let me stop a second.
(Beat.)
The story about those guys was actually a way to get to
another much more troubling encounter—speaking of
desire.

I have spent so much time talking about those stupid
jerks I won't have time to really explore this other
thing.
But please indulge me just a tiny bit longer. I'll finish
telling you what happened with those guys before we
leave, but this is the incident I...
we wanted to talk to you about.
Me and my collaborator.

Part 3

CASS: I was having a chat about all this with a theater
pal, Ahmed. The perils of being, of feeling like meat
sometimes.

Being a woman, etc. And he was telling me about the
coping strategies of women in his home country.

With veiling.

Different kinds of covering up, from head scarves, to covering up everything but the eyes. He said he was against that. Why should women have to cover up for what was really a guy's problem. "Women are being denied basic freedoms to deal with the weaknesses of men," he said. He got quite passionate. Angry at his own sex. The way their desires are always catered to. Even in this country. "You have a problem right here in the West," he said.

"Tell me about it," I said.

I also said veiling didn't feel like such a bad idea on some days, when I wish I could just pull the curtain down on myself. Those days when you don't want to be stared at. Wearing a burqa would feel like that Harry Potter's invisible cloak thing. Pft: vanish. What a relief. "No," he said, "wearing that only draws attention to yourself." And so on, a long night discussion. Anyway...

(She goes to the chair and puts on the dressing gown.)

We had several of these all-nighters. I thought he was very charming.

He had a modesty about him that I found appealing. The sort of person who could get passionate about things, but still have those strongly held beliefs sound as if they had a question mark about them. As in:

(Shaking her fist to demonstrate:)

"I really believe in what I'm saying, but should you disagree I am open to considering your argument; and maybe changing my mind about what a second ago sounded like a statement to end all statements."

Plus, he found me funny. The fact that he laughed at my jokes was a biggie. There's nothing like someone getting your humor to know this is someone you want to have stick around. If a guy gets you on that level, it's

like finding one big comfy chair that you can just plop
yourself into.

We also both worked in the theater.
Now this was a guy who knew his Ibsen from his
Beckett. It's so nice to be able to talk shop with
somebody who gets your references and silly theater
jokes.

And he had that gentle way of letting me know he was
attracted to me without pushing it. Which I suppose is
called flirting.

And I flirted right back. Did I mention I found him
attractive?

I did. There was this…

(Her hand touches her collar bone.)
part of his body that I—really found myself drawn to:
(Shows us:)
From his neck, over his collar bone, a little below, and
then to his broad shoulder.
When he was over in my studio one day, and it was
very humid, I said, "If you're boiling, take off your
shirt if you want to." Matter of factly. And he did.
He made a joke of taking it off. And I made a joke of
swooning.
(Traces her fingers over her collar bones, and shoulders.)
I really liked that area.—Weird, huh?
So there was an air of, a definite aura of—eroticism—in
the room.
And beyond our initial, "Oh, you're attractive"
moment, followed by, "Oh, you're of my tribe"
realization, where you see that the person shares the
same values and interests as you do, there was this—
you get on this—I guess it is called flirting.

Where you're still having the same conversation, but
now the words are dressed up a little differently. If you
know what I mean.
There's all this new body language that's now attached
to what you're saying.

And I, half unconsciously, engaged in my own
flirtatious ways. In the way you'll find yourself
reflexively doing things around people you find
attractive. You know, laughing a little too easily. I
personally start doing things with my shoulders that I
don't usually do—when I want to make a point. I sort
of scrunch it up to my chin; while I angle my face to
the shoulder,
(Demonstrates:)
in a sort of—I don't know what you'd call this. A sort
of sardonic "come hither" look? Heavy irony to mask
slightly embarrassing sexual desire? I'm not sure why
I'd think twisting myself up to look like I had some
neck and shoulder deformity would seem appealing.
But perhaps that was the point. To head off desire
at the gates. Keep it in check. "Fuck me" in heavy
quotation marks.

There's nothing nature seems to love more than the
mating dance.
And there's a moment in this—dance,
when the words you use become like—dummy lyrics,
if you will, to the tune that's really playing underneath.
You're talking to each other. But all real passion has
been drained from your words and now goes into this
other thing you're both feeling in your bodies.

And there's also this carelessness about how you
scatter your limbs—on a couch, or, wherever. Like
you're sort of letting them lie there like—bait? No.
Like you're pretending they don't quite have the same
moral agency you do.

They seem to have their own agenda.
You faintly acknowledge they're still yours,
but you disavow any responsibility for what they
might get up to. Should they misbehave. Like they're
props in this sexual drama that's heating up.

I am trying to be honest here.
I want to acknowledge my part in all this.
(*A moment as she tries to recollect*)
The thing is, I have a hard time remembering the
sequence of events.

As clearly as I remember every twitch and movement
of that encounter with those two guys on the street, I
can't quite put together everything that led up to this—
his,
um … what turned out to be his—insistence.
In the end.
I'm not sure when it crossed the line from a delicious—
from yielding to something that deeply wanted you.
That acknowledged you in ways you don't often
experience.
A desire that dug so deep into you that you felt like
shouting, YES, thank you. I'm not sure when—
when a "no",
when my "no" crept in.
I'm not sure when what had been so deeply invited by
me
felt—
disinvited.
When the clothes came off was fine.
That I remember ….
When we got into it was fine: Kissing, grabbing at each
other. Swallowing—
that's what it felt like—

swallowing each other's body with everything that
could swallow something, hands, lips, tongue, limbs
that wrapped around each other. Somewhere in that
encounter...
communication between two very articulate people—
broke down.

Somewhere,
not too long into it, I don't have a real sense of time
here, but it must have been in the first ten minutes?
More? I can't believe it was so soon. It seemed like
we were at it for a while ... where I started to feel—
uncomfortable.

It's tricky to talk about being uncomfortable in a
situation where there's already this sudden, and raw—
intimacy between two people who don't really know
each other.
Doing things we had never done together, naked. I
mean,
how do you pick out the uncomfortable moments from
the awkward ones that naturally happen in a situation
like that? How do you pick out the excitement of
jumping into the unknown from all that fumbling
around in the dark.

Personally, I kind of feel reluctant to speak up when
something isn't working for me. For instance:
As will happen sometimes,
a guy will go down on me,
and I won't know precisely what he's doing down
there.
I know what he's trying to do down there,
but sometimes it just isn't doing it for me.
Do I speak up in that moment? Do I start giving him
directions? No. I should. But I usually don't know the
guy well enough to fill him in on how best to work
my vagina. Getting through something as quickly as

possible is usually the simplest alternative. So I'll let
it go on for a couple of minutes, and then, when my
mind starts drifting into the merits of a Paleolithic diet,
for instance, I think, enough. I'll lift his head up to
make it seem like I want to gaze meaningfully into his
eyes, and we move on.

I mean,
we've got to have empathy here for each other—
in these vulnerable moments.
We make ourselves so vulnerable.
I know guys have body issues like women do. I
know they're trying to impress. I don't laugh when a
girlfriend talks about a guy's failure to launch. Gee,
I bet that was hilarious for the guy, and here you are
publicly humiliating him.
We are strangers enough to each other as it is.
We're trying. We're all trying to function as human
beings here and not be shown up for being bad at
something. I know others are much more demanding
about their needs, and good for them. For being clear
about what they want. Three cheers for the decisive
among us. Me? If you're fumbling towards me, if
you're making an ass of yourself doing so, but you're
coming from a good place, I'll be there for you. If I
know you're trying.

So when I became uncomfortable with what he was
doing, I made allowances.
When he became somewhat aggressive I interpreted it
as play. The take-charge approach. Okay. I can go with
that. Let's see where it goes. Because I *was* responding.
There was that "Yes, thank you" response in me
initially. I wasn't faking that. He did turn me on.
Until he—
wasn't anymore. And right there in that in-between—
(*Trying to find the words*)

chunk of—love-making, that went from love-making
to—not love, where…
(Trying to find the words)
I felt I wasn't part of—that I wasn't there for him
anymore.
I don't know where I went. It was like I'd all but
disappeared. I was there,
then I wasn't.
My great vanishing act.
Abracadabra, poof.
I was disappearing in all his—neediness; and pawing.
The person he'd been chatting with was like—. I had
somehow exited the room and there was just this—
body of mine to take. And my voice must have been
this far off thing because he didn't seem to hear me
when I said stop. Though he says I didn't say stop. I
know I tried to push him away, which he thought was
play, but I'm sure I said stop. My body was saying it
for sure. I think it was pretty much screaming it at one
point. I think I was screaming it. Was I? I still,
it's still—
I still don't know how two very articulate people,
who got each other so well, could find themselves
suddenly unable to speak to each other.

I am pretty sure I said stop….
I know I was confused for a time. About what was—
how it flipped. I can't quite piece together that—
grey area. But whatever the sequence,
after a while, I sort of went—
limp.
(A moment)
After he finished,
we lay there.

I thought, this is not quite—

I'm not quite…
I'm not—
all together here.

I lay there,
waiting for the parts that seemed to have gone missing,
to come back. To all come back to earth in one piece.
To all come back to me and make me
of a piece.

He didn't say anything.
That felt very pointed.
Then he got up and peed.
He came back, got into bed. Leant over me. And—
smiled.
Like he was back.
Like the person I had fallen for—
was back.
Looking at me.

Where did you go?

You haven't properly explained it to me even now.
Because when I looked in your eyes during that—when
things flipped—you seemed to have exited the room as
well. Lights on but no one home.
I still don't understand what you think happened but
it wasn't—by no stretch of the imagination did it have
anything to do with love. It may have started that way,
but it ended up in the arctic end of something horribly
cold and not—
not love.

After your smile…

it was that smile that got me out of bed.
I dressed without saying anything.
Which confused you. I don't remember what you said.
I wasn't absorbing much of anything at that point. I do

remember the concern in your voice. Then the panic
as I got dressed without saying anything. As I got my
things together.
The things that could be collected.
And left…

There were calls, texts, e-mails from you.
I never responded.

About a year later, we found ourselves in the same
production. You as assistant director. We spoke as
professionals when we had to. I caught you looking at
me a few times. Like you were still trying to figure out
what happened.
One time after rehearsal, when the cast and crew were
hanging out in a bar, we ended up alone when the
group we were with decided to call it a night.

It was then that it occurred to me:
Maybe you'd concluded that I just must be one of those
crazy, artist types. Flighty; neurotic; irrational.
Female.
It probably had nothing to do with you.
It was me. Maybe that's how you'd processed that
night.
So when you decided to gingerly bring up the subject,
looking down at your beer, I told you:

"Just to be clear: whatever it started out as, it ended up
as a rape."

You looked at me like you hadn't heard me properly.
I repeated it. More shock.
Eyes wide; your face sweating.
I decided to let that hang and see what you'd say.
When you said, "What?"
I said, "Would you like me to say it louder so the
whole room can hear?"

"Cass…Cass."

I said, "I never want to be alone in the same room with you again." And left.

We couldn't leave it there, of course.
Not only because we continued to see each other in rehearsals. I had questions.
I needed to know what happened. And the only way I could get any answers would be to—make myself vulnerable again.
It's strange how that works. How any real answers to anything,
any real knowledge, any real love, can only happen to the degree you're prepared to leave yourself wide open—to possibly being hurt. Maybe that's why in fairy tales little girls are always approaching monsters for answers.

Plus the artist in me, the part that can hover over even my own pain, that part wanted to ask:

"What the fuck were you thinking?"

So I did allow myself to be alone with him again one night after rehearsal.

When he saw I was giving him an opening to speak, he took it. He said he was mortified. Beyond mortified. He didn't believe I was speaking about him. "In a million years I wouldn't so much as think of causing you pain," he said. I repeat his words and the way he said them as honestly as I can remember. You said:

"I have been going over and over that night trying to figure out what I did and I am—so, so sorry. I don't want to try and explain or excuse myself. It'll just seem like I'm trying to justify what can't be justified—if something did happen. And if you say it did, it did. I know I didn't intend it, God how could I. But that's not the point. Your experience of it is what matters. There can be no other side, no other voice in this. But in spite

of that, I have to say something or I'll go mad thinking
about this. Cass, I thought you were—enjoying
yourself. I kept thinking this is great. We get on, we're
compatible, we get each other. I thought you were into
it. The only thing that I can think of is, maybe—I—you
were so sexy, and I—your body was so amazing and
I just, maybe for a moment—I paid more attention to
how I was enjoying myself,
and not how you were responding.
I've always made sure the woman is satisfied before I
am. Which is why I can't believe I could have mistaken
your hating it for pleasure.
And now to be accused of behaving in a way that
would make me scream if I heard this about another
man. That's like a waking nightmare. Like I've woken
up in the body of a criminal."

"That's what's so scary, Ahmed," I said.
I went to bed with one person,
and then someone else showed up.
And whoever took over didn't seem to notice me at
all."
"No. I saw nothing but you," he said.
"I was lost in you.
I—
disappeared in you."
(Beat)

The more he spoke, the more hysterical his grief
became. He said he would do anything I wanted him
to do. I told him I wasn't going to report him to the
police. He insisted it had nothing to do with that.
I asked him if I could contact a couple of his ex's. I
wanted to know if this had happened before. He gave
me their contact information.
I haven't contacted them yet ….

There's something that happens when someone
searches deep in your eyes, like he was doing,
as he tries to figure out what your next move might be.
As it relates to his future.
Like a dog who looks up to its owner to see what their
next command might be.
I have to confess that gave me some satisfaction.
That I had that over him.
Then it creeped me out that I was getting off on that.
Then I gave myself permission to get off on it as a way
to feel a little better.
There were other factors I won't get into, like his
being a recent immigrant, which he threw out as an
aside, without meaning it to be an excuse, but that's
exactly what he was implying. That maybe I had
misinterpreted his actions because they were coming
from someone associated with a part of the world
that's supposed to be hard on women.
I just gave that a cold stare and he backed down.
But then I said, "Well, maybe you thought that
because I was an American I would be extra slutty and
amenable to shit like that."
A horrified "no" from him and more hysterical
pleading.
Then,
I have to admit,
another train of thought:
I wondered if it had been a rape after all.
I couldn't name it when it was happening.
So maybe it wasn't.
Maybe I was just a slut.
An accidental slut.
During those times when I'm not on heightened alert
for signs I may be giving off.

But then I had to wonder what being a slut meant
exactly. Because slut in that case would just be me,
being myself,
relaxed, not having to be responsible for how you react
to me. Not being responsible for your weaknesses,
like you said. As if being sexual was like having rabies,
or something, that some poor guy might catch just by
looking at me. At which point he is not responsible for
his actions.

And even if I was a slut, how does rape follow from
that?

But then, who am I to think I live in a vacuum? Who
am I to think I can control the attention I sometimes
seek.

So I went to you and said, "I can't unfeel what I'm
feeling. You can't undo what you did. I can't let go of
something I haven't been able to wrap my arms around
in the first place. The thing you say didn't happen.
But here I am in the grip of something I don't know the
shape of, or soul of. So let's do what we do.
Let's explore it.
We're theater people.
You want to be a director. I'm also a writer.
I'll write.
You'll direct.
We'll collaborate.

I promise it won't be an indictment.
I won't attack you in public.
I just need to figure out what happened.

I want to know if I'm responsible for any of this. If I'm
sending out—
I don't know what,

for these kinds of things to come into my life. That I
absolutely don't want in my life. Am I collaborating in
that too?

You said it would be inappropriate to direct me.
Given the power dynamic between director and
performer, giving me directions; telling me how to
move. "I can never again put myself in a position
where you don't have full control," you said, rather
academically. I said I will have full control. I will be in
charge of this. There will always be a stage manager
present. We will never be alone. I just want you to tell
me if you can hear me at the back.

What I most want from you is to hear me struggle to
get to the bottom of this. I want you to listen to me.
And watch.
If you care. If you're as empathetic as you say you are.
I want you to hear me wrestle this fucking thing to the
ground. Over and over; every time we rehearse this,
every time I fucking perform it. I want you to witness
what you apparently couldn't see when we were in
bed together.

And it won't just be about you.
It will also be about a woman walking down the street
at night. Seeing two guys up ahead. And how very
threatened she felt by that.

About those guys…
one of whom wanted to be sucked off.
I dodged that bullet when I saw a cop car rolling up
behind them.
I walked towards it,
through them again,
giving him hope for all of two seconds before he saw
where I was heading. They skipped out of there while I
pretended to ask the cop for directions.

The cop himself stared at me like, What are you doing
out here at night dressed like that? Don't you know
you're asking for trouble.
(A moment, then:)

I keep coming back to that first kiss…
With that boy on the porch.
The kiss I fantasized about experiencing for so long.
How very far away we seemed to be as we both leant
in for
the beginning of…
everything.
How for ever it felt before our lips
met. And when they did,
how perfect it was. Not awkward like some people
say their first kisses are. No. This was even better than
I hoped. His lips were…lovely. My lips landed on his
like—
bee pollen.
Then like naked feet in wet sand.
Curling my toes into moist sand.
Pressing our soft lips together.
That unbelievable sensation. And the certainty,
that with this first kiss—
this was going to be the start of wonderful things to
follow.
The very first, and amazing step of becoming a fully
grown-up woman.
And all the adventures that lay ahead.

(Hold for a beat. Blackout)

END OF PLAY

www.ingramcontent.com/pod-product-compliance
Lightning Source LLC
Chambersburg PA
CBHW070035110426
42741CB00035B/2779